# Waiting in Joyful Hope

*Daily Reflections for
Advent and Christmas
2016–2017*

Robert F. Morneau

**LITURGICAL PRESS**

Collegeville, Minnesota

www.litpress.org

*Nihil Obstat:* Reverend Robert Harren, J.C.L., *Censor deputatus.*
*Imprimatur:* ✠ Most Reverend Donald J. Kettler, J.C.L., Bishop of Saint Cloud, Minnesota. March 24, 2016.

Cover design by Monica Bokinskie. Cover photo © Thinkstock.

ISSN: 1550-803X
ISBN: 978-0-8146-4864-3    978-0-8146-4890-2 (ebook)

# Introduction

I have been a member of a book club for over twenty years. One of our members has the ability to summarize a book, be it Thomas Merton's *New Seeds of Contemplation* or John Wooden's *A Game Plan for Life: The Power of Mentoring* or Christian Wiman's *Ambition and Survival*, in three or four paragraphs. He goes to the heart of the matter and summarizes the core ideas and meanings.

My practice, though much less successful, is to summarize a book in the form of a poem. After reading Pope Francis's apostolic exhortation *The Joy of the Gospel* (*Evangelii Gaudium*), I came up with these lines:

### The Joy of the Gospel

When the message of divine Love is heard,
when that Love is lived and shared,
when words of tenderness are spoken
and deeds of kindness expressed,
we have entered the field of evangelization.

In that field there is truth and beauty,
goodness and joy, zeal and enthusiasm.
In that field hope blossoms, trust too.
The mandate is clear, unambiguous—
"Go forth! Leave your security behind
and your comfort. Yes, go tell it on the mountain."

Pope Francis issued this exhortation just before Advent in 2013. The focus calls us to be evangelizers, venturing forth to tell the good news on the mountains and in the valleys, on street corners and in bars, at the kitchen table and at wedding receptions. The pope reminds us that the message of evangelization never changes: "The heart of its message will always be the same: the God who revealed his immense love in the crucified and risen Christ" (11). Advent once again puts us in touch with *the* message.

Another Advent theme in *Evangelii Gaudium* deals with the Emmanuel factor, that God is truly with us in Jesus. Pope Francis says, "A true missionary, who never ceases to be a disciple, knows that Jesus walks with him, speaks to him, breathes with him, works with him" (266). Through baptism we are disciples and missionaries, called to go forth. But we are not alone. Because of the Christmas mystery, we believe that the Bethlehem Jesus who came so many years ago is also the Easter Christ, risen and accompanying us on our pilgrim journey. Herein is our trust and faith.

Toward the end of his exhortation, Pope Francis speaks of "the revolutionary nature of love and tenderness" (288). Advent is a season of love, God's love made visible in Jesus. Advent is a season of tenderness, an awareness that God's love and mercy is revealed in Christ whose heart is filled with affection and gentleness. And one last word from our Holy Father: "No single act of love for God will be lost, no generous effort is meaningless, no painful endurance is wasted" (279). Advent is truly a season of joy, a joy that comes to us through the Gospel.

# FIRST WEEK OF ADVENT

*November 27: First Sunday of Advent*

## Master Teachers

**Readings:** Isa 2:1-5; Rom 13:11-14; Matt 24:37-44

**Scripture:**
Let us then throw off the works of darkness
 and put on the armor of light;
 let us conduct ourselves properly as in the day . . .
  (Rom 13:12b-13a)

**Reflection:** Isaiah, St. Paul, and Jesus were all on the same page: the coming of God's grace here and now. With images and examples, they urged their audience to be alert and awake to God's nearness. With urgency, they prodded their people to leave the land of darkness and sin, and to walk in the light of day.

Isaiah is a master teacher. His lesson plan is clear and direct: we all need to be instructed in God's way and walk in God's path. Only by walking in God's light will wars end and peace be experienced. And then that powerful image of the transformation of swords and spears, the first into plowshares, the second into pruning hooks. As pilgrims we are on a journey toward the mountain, toward God's mountain of peace and joy.

St. Paul is also a master teacher, spelling out in detail those behaviors and attitudes that thwart salvation: orgies and drunkenness, lust and promiscuity, rivalry and jealousy.

From experience Paul knew well that it is in the person of Christ that we are given the light to see what really matters, and the grace to do the Father's will. Like Isaiah, Paul will not accept procrastination. The hour is now; the day is at hand; wake up!

Jesus is *the* master teacher, instructing us not only in word but by his living out the Father's will. Jesus urges his disciples to be prepared, ready to welcome the movement of grace in their hearts. Getting caught up in eating and drinking, in a life of self-indulgence, deadens one's sensitivity even to the point of sleepwalking. Would that our soul had an alarm system to keep us alert. Maybe it does, our conscience.

A master teacher and influential theologian of the recent past was Fr. Bernard Lonergan (d. 1984). His first imperative for authentic human living was "Be attentive!"

It is only by staying awake, being alert, practicing attentiveness that we are able to respond to the unexpected comings of our Lord.

**Meditation:** Who are the master teachers in your life? What have they taught you? What have you taught others about our journey of faith?

**Prayer:** Lord Jesus, as we begin our Advent season, give us the energy and courage to stay awake and respond to your slightest nudge. Protect us from insensitivity; grace us with the desire to walk in the light of your love. Come, Lord Jesus, come.

## Amazing Faith/Amazing Grace

**Readings:** Isa 4:2-6; Matt 8:5-11

**Scripture:**
The centurion said in reply,
   "Lord, I am not worthy to have you enter under my roof;
   only say the word and my servant will be healed."
   (Matt 8:8)

**Reflection:** In just seven verses of today's gospel we learn quite a bit about the anonymous centurion: he was a man of compassion, a person who understood how authority works, and an individual of deep faith. Jesus was *amazed* at the centurion's conviction that he, Jesus, could heal and, yes, heal from a distance. A simple word would do it.

Back in 1994, hundreds of thousands of people were killed in a genocide in Rwanda. One individual who barely escaped told the story of what happened to her and her family. Her name is Immaculée Ilibagiza and her 2006 book is *Left to Tell: Discovering God Amidst the Rwandan Holocaust*. For ninety-one days, she and seven women companions hid in a small bathroom to escape the genocide killers. Immaculée came out of the ordeal exemplifying an incredible faith: she forgave the people who killed her parents, two brothers, and many other friends and relatives. Many who read the book or have heard her speak come away feeling, like Jesus, *amazed*.

During Advent we are preparing to celebrate the amazing grace of God's love, a love made manifest and present in the mystery of the nativity of our Lord. We might ask for an early Christmas present, the gift of amazing faith. This faith, once appropriated, empowers us to believe in Jesus' healing power; this faith, once assimilated, empowers us to forgive those who hurt us and even to forgive ourselves if need be. Hopefully, though we are no longer children, we have not lost the ability to be amazed.

**Meditation:** What is your level of amazement? What is your level of faith? In what sense do these two dispositions impact one another?

**Prayer:** Loving God, in the face of illness and suffering, grant us the gift of compassion. And when we find it hard to believe and live your word, deepen our faith and trust. Though Christmas is far off, we ask for an early gift that, if given, we will share with others.

## Being Seen/Seeing

**Readings:** Isa 11:1-10; Luke 10:21-24

**Scripture:**
[Jesus said,] "For I say to you,
  many prophets and kings desired to see what you see,
  but did not see it,
  and to hear what you hear, but did not hear it."
    (Luke 10:24)

**Reflection:** St. John of the Cross (1542–91), the great Carmelite mystic and Doctor of the Church, writes about God's gaze, God looking at us. Saint John maintains that four effects follow from being seen by God: God's look cleanses and enriches us, endows us with grace and enlightens us. Being seen by God transforms us.

Isaiah has the same message as John. The Old Testament prophet tells us that when the Spirit of the Lord comes upon us many gifts are bestowed: wisdom and understanding, counsel and strength, knowledge and fear of the Lord. These gifts enrich and cleanse us, endow us with grace and illumine our journey.

In Thornton Wilder's play *Our Town* (1938), there is a scene in which a main character, Emily, dead some fourteen years, returns to earth and addresses her mother with a simple plea, namely, that they "look" at one another. The playwright has a message for the audience: too seldom do we really look and see one another, and that is a tragedy.

Advent is a time to be seen and to see, to be loved and to love. God's gaze is transformative but we must be willing to embrace that look. Kings and prophets, in their own mysterious way, yearned to see and hear what the disciples of Jesus saw and heard—God's abiding love in Jesus. Deep down those kings and prophets and all of us do not really yearn to see and hear so much as to be seen and to be heard.

**Meditation:** What happens to your heart when you are looked at in a loving way? When you look at others is it a stare and critical analysis, or is it a childlike look of affection?

**Prayer:** Lord Jesus, bless our eyes and our ears, our minds and our hearts, so that we might truly be your disciples and walk in your way. As we pray in the gospel acclamation, "Behold, our Lord shall come with power; / he will enlighten the eyes of his servants." Come, Lord Jesus, come.

*November 30:*
*Saint Andrew, Apostle* (Catholic Church)

*Wednesday of the First Week of Advent*
(Episcopal Church)

## Cabela's and the Kingdom

**Readings:** Rom 10:9-18; Matt 4:18-22

**Scripture:**
He [Jesus] said to them [Simon and Andrew],
   "Come after me, and I will make you fishers of men."
At once they left their nets and followed him.
   (Matt 4:19-20)

**Reflection:** Recently a huge hunting and fishing store, Cabela's by name, came to our community. Many outdoors people consider it to be the mecca in their field. Thousands of people have traveled great distances since the message has gone out that Cabela's is in town. Fishermen and hunters abandon the workplace and their homes and immediately buy new equipment. Fish and deer, beware!

Jesus' store, the Kingdom, arrived in Galilee. His merchandise did not include boats and guns and fly rods, but love and mercy and compassion. Not many applied for a job to engage in this enterprise, but several did. And their commitment was astounding: abandonment of nets and boats, of fathers and families. Andrew, the brother of Simon Peter, was one of them.

**12**   *First Week of Advent*

Andrew, like the other eleven disciples, as well as St. Paul, would eventually merit Isaiah's assertion: "How beautiful upon the mountains / are the feet of the one bringing good news" (Isa 52:7). The good news is a person, Jesus the Christ. In him, we see God's love and mercy manifest; in him, we are offered the gift of faith.

Let us not think that Jesus entrusted the coming of the kingdom to just a few fishermen. All of us, through baptism, are evangelists, carrying the good news to every segment of society. If our ears are attuned, each morning we will hear the Lord's call: "Come after me!"

**Meditation:** How "immediate" is your response to God's morning call to follow in his way? Who are the individuals, whose feet are beautiful as Isaiah says, who have brought to you the good news?

**Prayer:** Jesus, Fisher of men and women, of saints and sinners, of prophets and princes, help us to jump into your net. For too long we have been elusive, running from your word and your demands. May this Advent be a time of coming home into the glory of your love.

## A Spiritual Gibraltar: Faith

**Readings:** Isa 26:1-6; Matt 7:21, 24-27

**Scripture:**
Trust in the LORD forever!
   For the LORD is an eternal Rock. (Isa 26:4)

**Reflection:** Driving across the Golden Gate Bridge demands implicit trust. Drivers assume that the architect and the construction workers knew what they were doing. Solid foundations were laid and safety was assured (hopefully).

God, the Divine Architect, has designed a world that merits our confidence. As long as we listen and follow God's commandments, our lives will rest on an everlasting rock. Failure to hear and obey means sure ruin.

Some cultures put their trust in horses and chariots, in drones and bombs, in financial portfolios and diplomas on the wall, in fame and fortune. Building the house of our soul on such precarious entities demonstrates a lack of wisdom. It is God's word, heard and heeded, that gives us graced stability.

Faith is our option for solid footings. Another choice might be to seek security in annuities, mutual funds, real estate, insurance policies. One of the Fortune Global 500 companies is The Prudential Insurance Company of America. Their logo is the Rock of Gibraltar and the company attempts to attract customers with the slogan "Own a Piece of the Rock."

Financial security is a valid need. So too is spiritual security. Each of us has to decide on what or whom we will build our spiritual security.

**Meditation:** Can you recall the times you built your decisions and commitments on sand? on firm foundations? What is your understanding of why Jesus decided to select Peter as the one (the Rock) on whom the foundation of the church would be entrusted?

**Prayer:** Gracious God, give us the wisdom to make good decisions. Too often our values are far too sandy. Only through the gift of your Holy Spirit will we be able to construct our lives on virtues that lead to love, joy, and peace.

## Red-Letter Days

**Readings:** Isa 29:17-24; Matt 9:27-31

**Scripture:**
Those who err in spirit shall acquire understanding,
   and those who find fault shall receive instruction.
      (Isa 29:24)

**Reflection:** St. Paul, when Saul, was dead wrong. He found fault with the early Christians; he erred in misunderstanding the Christian faith. He was blind, literally for several days, until Christ, the Son of David, had pity on him. The words of "Amazing Grace" would become Paul's own: "I once was lost, but now am found, / Was blind, but now I see."

Teachers have those red-letter days when, after months of teaching, a student yells out: "Now I see!" A paraphrase: "Now I understand the Pythagorean theory, or Einstein's theory of relativity, or the makeup of DNA!" Acquisition of understanding is truly to be treasured. And yet, St. Paul writes, "Then the peace of God that surpasses all understanding will guard your hearts and minds in Christ Jesus" (Phil 4:7). As great as understanding and wisdom are, they cannot be compared with the peace of Christ. What peace the two blind men in today's gospel experienced when Jesus touched their eyes and gave them sight.

Paul found fault with the Christian community but then the risen Christ instructed him in *the* way, the way of discipleship. Paul would go on to instruct others in the way of truth. We are the recipients of his instructions: "Bear one another's burdens, and so you will fulfill the law of Christ" (Gal 6:2); "[Give] thanks always and for everything in the name of our Lord Jesus Christ to God the Father" (Eph 5:20).

Error and faults! Understanding and instruction! As pilgrims we need saints and theologians to correct our mistakes and to overcome our faults. We need the Lord Jesus to come once again, during these Advent days, to instruct us in the paths of his Father.

**Meditation:** Are you experienced in finding faults with those around you and with our country and church? What was the greatest error in your life? Who were the people who instructed you and gave you understanding regarding the meaning of life?

**Prayer:** Lord Jesus, we long to see and hear your word. Cure our blindness; heal our arrogance and pride. Give us the faith to follow your call to be beloved sons and daughters of your Father. With eyes and ears open, we will proclaim your praise.

*December 3:*
*Saint Francis Xavier, Priest* (Catholic Church)

*Saturday of the First Week of Advent*
(Episcopal Church)

## To Give or Not to Give: That Is the Question

**Readings:** Isa 30:19-21, 23-26; Matt 9:35–10:1, 5a, 6-8

**Scripture:**
"Without cost you have received; without cost you are to
give." (Matt 10:8b)

**Reflection:** "There ain't no free lunches," so the saying goes.
Yet there is another refrain in the background: "The best
things in life are free!" We seem to have here Charles Dick-
ens's paradox of living in the best and the worst of times. So
which way is it? Is everything we have and are the result of
our labor and self-sufficiency, or is a huge portion of life
sheer gift, sheer grace?

The facts are fairly clear: sunshine and rain are free. So too
the air we breathe and the gravity that holds us in place. Add
to this God's grace—God's light, love, and life—that we paid
nothing for. Hopefully our response is one of profound gratitude; hopefully we take nothing for granted—all is gift. The
psalmist puts the cards on the table: "How can I repay the
LORD / for all the great good done for me?" (Ps 116:12).

During Advent some parishes have a "Giving Tree" from
which dangle numerous tags for parishioners to take and

return. On the tags are requests for a food or gas card for those in need. This ministry provides an opportunity to get caught up in the giving process, taking what we have and sharing it with others. As we become "empty," space is created for a new influx of God's grace, be it material or spiritual. And it is amazing what joy fills the heart when generosity becomes a way of life.

**Meditation:** What have you been freely given? What have you freely given in return? Why is hoarding and accumulating so injurious to the spiritual life?

**Prayer:** God of generosity, may we emulate you in passing on to others a portion of the gifts you have given to us. In giving we experience Advent joy; in giving we are true to our being made in the image and likeness of you. Keep greed far from our hearts, Lord. Help us to experience the graced poverty of being open to your coming.

# SECOND WEEK OF ADVENT

*December 4: Second Sunday of Advent*

## Advent's Urgency: Repent

**Readings:** Isa 11:1-10; Rom 15:4-9; Matt 3:1-12

**Scripture:**
John the Baptist appeared, preaching in the desert of Judea
and saying, "Repent, for the kingdom of heaven is at
hand!" (Matt 3:1-2)

**Reflection:** In a poem titled "Halo Effect," the poet Marilyn
Chandler McIntyre reflects on revelation, conversion, and
epiphany. Her "preaching," like John the Baptist, makes the
claim that grace, God's light and presence, is always present.
Our challenge is to be awake and attentive to the kingdom
that is at hand.

However, a proper disposition is needed to be present to
reality. Unless there is some degree of interior change (let's
call it "repentance" or change of mind and heart), we miss
so much of life and the workings of grace. Preoccupation
with oneself (narcissism), having too many things to do (ac-
tivism), or simply insensitivity lead to a narrow existence.
John the Baptist challenges us to wake up, as do all prophets
and poets.

What is this kingdom of heaven? Isaiah the prophet describes certain attributes that indicate that God's reign is at
hand, indeed, present in the here and now. God's rule is
manifest in righteousness and fidelity, in those who have

wisdom and understanding, in the women and men who have knowledge and fear of the Lord. When peace replaces hostility, when trust drives out anxiety, when hope displaces despair, the kingdom of God is present.

By contrast, John Cassian, a Christian monk and theologian, describes the kingdom of the devil as one of unrighteousness and discord, death-dealing gloom and lifelessness. When these qualities are present in our individual lives or in our culture, the need for repentance is urgent.

Our hope in this Advent season is grounded in St. Paul's reminder that our God is a God of steadfastness and encouragement. In the call to repentance and conversion, God does not want us to become discouraged. Rather, we are to trust that Jesus, the faithful Son, has been given to us. We are not alone in our striving to be faithful to our baptism call. Saint Paul would have us rejoice always in the Lord.

**Meditation:** What are the areas in your life (attitudes, dispositions, behavior) that the Lord is calling you to address in this Advent season? Saint Paul tells us that God's kingdom is about righteousness, peace, and joy (Rom 14:17). In what way are you an instrument of peace and joy to others?

**Prayer:** Loving God, as we pray "Thy kingdom come," grant us the courage to follow your Son Jesus in being a channel of your peace and joy. Enlighten us to see those areas of our life that need transformation. May we feel the urgency of the Baptist's message that we repent, for your kingdom is indeed at hand.

*December 5: Monday of the Second Week of Advent*

## Go Home

**Readings:** Isa 35:1-10; Luke 5:17-26

**Scripture:**
"But that you may know
    that the Son of Man has authority on earth to forgive
        sins"—
    he said to the one who was paralyzed,
    "I say to you, rise, pick up your stretcher, and go home."
        (Luke 5:24)

**Reflection:** One of the constant refrains in the gospel is "Come, follow me!" Mother Teresa of Calcutta heard that call in September of 1948 and she never looked back (unlike poor Lot's wife). Peter and Andrew, James and John left their nets and boats and pursued Jesus. Seldom do we hear Jesus telling people to go home.

Yet, in this healing miracle the paralyzed man did go home, as Jesus instructed, carrying his stretcher. We can only imagine what awaited him there. An astonished wife? Children who now had a healthy father? Neighbors amazed to see the once paralyzed man walking and glorifying God? Evangelization is as important on the home front as it is in the foreign missions. Each of us is given a unique call.

And what about the men who carried the paralyzed man to Jesus? They were men of faith, a faith that impressed Jesus.

They were also sinners. "When Jesus saw *their* faith, he said, 'As for you, your sins are forgiven'" (Luke 5:20). Healing came both to the paralytic and to his friends. We witness here a physical and spiritual healing.

And the poor scribes and Pharisees! Little did they realize how God's forgiveness works. With all their book learning and theological reflections, they didn't get it. So Jesus "had" to astonish them into how God's forgiveness is mediated in so many ways. Those scribes and Pharisees would have a hard time accepting the sacrament of reconciliation.

**Meditation:** What has been your experience of physical and spiritual healing? How did that healing come to you? In what ways have you extended forgiveness to others and how have you brought healing to the lives of your family and friends?

**Prayer:** Lord Jesus, we all have our stretchers because sin does paralyze and hold us in bondage. Free us from our addictions; forgive our sins; restore us to our families and friends. Send us home and then out into the highways and byways glorifying your power and mercy.

*December 6: Tuesday of the Second Week of Advent*

## "I Once Was Lost . . ."

**Readings:** Isa 40:1-11; Matt 18:12-14

**Scripture:**
Like a shepherd he feeds his flock;
   in his arms he gathers the lambs,
Carrying them in his bosom,
   and leading the ewes with care. (Isa 40:11)

**Reflection:** Shepherds have quite a task: feeding, gathering, carrying, leading the flock. But there is yet another duty: seeking out and finding the lost sheep.

Few of us on this perilous journey of life have not been lost at one time or another. Sometimes it happens in seventh grade or as a junior in high school. Sometimes we get lost because of unemployment or difficulties in marriage. Sometimes we get lost because of our poor choices or lack of self-care.

Blessed are those who are gifted with a "good shepherd" who appears just at the right time. It might be a compassionate teacher, a caring counselor, a sensitive coworker, a forgiving spouse. God sends people into our lives to offer us encouragement or a safe haven.

The wandering and lost Augustine was given Ambrose; Dante was gifted with Virgil; the disciples had Jesus. We dare not travel alone even if we own a GPS. We are social creatures and stand in need of companionship. Technology may help to save our physical lives but it cannot save our souls.

One might question the wisdom of leaving the ninety-nine in search of the one. God's wisdom is not ours. We play it safe, whereas God will risk everything for the salvation of a single person.

**Meditation:** Who are the "saviors" in your life? Whom have you sought out and found? What does the first stanza of "Amazing Grace" say about your life?

**Prayer:** Jesus, our good shepherd, do not let us stray from you or one another. Teach us to stay close to you through the sacraments and your holy word. Give us the courage to reach out to those who are struggling and who dwell on the margins. May we welcome them into our hearts as you welcomed us into your loving embrace.

*December 7:*
*Saint Ambrose, Bishop and Doctor of the Church*
(Catholic Church)

*Wednesday of the Second Week of Advent*
(Episcopal Church)

## Loneliness: Long and Hard

**Readings:** Isa 40:25-31; Matt 11:28-30

**Scripture:**
Why, O Jacob, do you say,
    and declare, O Israel,
"My way is hidden from the LORD,
    and my right is disregarded by my God"? (Isa 40:27)

**Reflection:** *The Long Loneliness: The Autobiography of Dorothy Day* tells the story of a woman deeply concerned about human rights and justice. It also describes our human condition, our loneliness and fears, our struggle for freedom and peace. Deep down Dorothy Day knew that God did not disregard her plight nor was she able to hide her ways from the Lord.

Jesus, in the wonder of his self-emptying love (kenosis), knew from the inside the long loneliness of our human pilgrimage. He experienced hunger and thirst, love and rejection, friendship and betrayal, great joy and sorrows, yes, life and death. Jesus knew how burdensome work can be, how heavy the yoke of human existence, the importance of humility and meekness. Ours is not an outsider God; in Jesus our God tasted everything but sin.

An Advent practice that prepares us well for the nativity of the Lord is that of encouragement. Because life can be filled with loneliness and hardship, everyone needs to be encouraged to persevere in our following of Christ. To be an agent of encouragement is to be an instrument of God's grace. Just as God cheers us on, that we might soar like an eagle, so we too are to cheer others on in the darkness of these Advent days.

**Meditation:** Who are the people in your life who need encouragement? In what ways can you cheer them on lest they falter?

**Prayer:** God of encouragement, we stand in need of your supportive hand. When loneliness sets in, may we turn to you for assistance and reach out to others who carry heavy burdens. With you sharing our yoke, we can do great things.

*December 8:*
*Immaculate Conception of the Blessed Virgin Mary*
(Catholic Church)

*Thursday of the Second Week of Advent*
(Episcopal Church)

## "How Can I Keep from Singing?"

**Readings:** Gen 3:9-15, 20; Eph 1:3-6, 11-12; Luke 1:26-38

**Scripture:**
Sing to the Lord a new song, for he has done marvelous
   deeds. (Ps 98:1)

**Reflection:** When marvelous deeds are done, when we celebrate someone's birthday, when Olympic athletes receive
their medals, music fills the air, be it a national anthem, our
traditional birthday song, or a glorious alleluia. As the great
spiritual hymn goes, "How can I keep from singing?"

On this feast of Mary, her Immaculate Conception, the
great story of the annunciation is told once again. This marvelous deed of God, the Word becoming flesh in the womb
of Mary, is a scandal to the secular world. But to people of
faith, this event gives us blessed assurance of God's extrava-
gant love. How fitting it is that the focus of our Christian
faith is on the Lord. Even though our feast today celebrates
Mary's conception, the gospel passage directs our attention
to Jesus' conception and the working of the Holy Spirit. Mary
would have it no other way.

In speaking of the conceptions of Jesus and Mary, we are in the land of mystery. A narrow rationalism has no way of dealing with the claims of faith. And even for believers, our minds are too finite and limited to comprehend these two conceptions. So we break into song, singing our theology, for again, how is it possible to stop from singing when God is about his business of manifesting his love?

Raïssa Maritain, the wife of the noted philosopher Jacques Maritain, wrote a journal. One of her entries dealt with song and how necessary singing is to express love. Her claim is that speech, the spoken word, is simply "too arid, too narrow" to articulate love, be it God's love for us or our love for God and one another.

The psalmist's imperative gives us the reason for our singing: "Sing to the Lord a new song, for he has done marvelous deeds" (Ps 98:1).

**Meditation:** What role does music play in your faith life? What role does Mary have in your Christian discipleship?

**Prayer:** Mary, our mentor and model, help us to sing the Lord's praises; help us to have the holy obedience that you lived.

*December 9: Friday of the Second Week of Advent*

## Eating/Drinking: Yes/No

**Readings:** Isa 48:17-19; Matt 11:16-19

**Scripture:**
"For John came neither eating nor drinking, and they said,
  'He is possessed by a demon.'" (Matt 11:18)

**Reflection:** St. Paul, following in the way of Jesus, was concerned about the kingdom of God. In writing to the Romans (14:17), Paul makes it abundantly clear that God's reign is about justice, peace, and joy; it is not about eating or drinking.

John the Baptist focused on pointing out that Jesus was the Lamb of God who took away our sins and the one who made manifest God's love for us. John found asceticism to be important in fulfilling his ministry. Fasting kept his mind clear and his heart energized to follow his calling as a prophet, as God's faithful messenger.

Jesus' mission was to proclaim the kingdom of God. His Father was to reign in the hearts and minds of people so that they might live in love and truth. So Jesus ate and drank with all kinds of people, saints and sinners. It was at table that he looked into their eyes and, in that glance, transformed them. Eating and drinking created fellowship at table and gave entrance into peoples' lives.

So what are we to do in this Advent season? Eat and drink, fast and do penance? It is not an either/or situation. If the flute is being played, we dance. At Christmas parties and wedding celebrations we eat and drink in moderation. If a dirge sounds, we mourn the loss of a loved one or repent of our sins by doing penance, by practicing asceticism. In the end what matters is justice, peace, and joy flowing from a loving heart; what matters is not having a steak and a glass of wine, as pleasant as that might be.

**Meditation:** What are your eating and drinking patterns? On Ash Wednesday, we were told to pray, fast, and give alms. During this Advent do you have any fasting practices?

**Prayer:** Lord Jesus, you come to eat and drink with us in the Eucharist. You come to call us to be agents of justice, peace, and joy. We also hear your call to discipline, to order our lives so as to further the growth of the kingdom. Grace us to do the Father's will.

## Fire and Ice

**Readings:** Sir 48:1-4, 9-11; Matt 17:9a, 10-13

**Scripture:**
In those days,
like a fire there appeared the prophet Elijah
   whose words were as a flaming furnace. (Sir 48:1)

**Reflection:** In his poem "Fire and Ice," Robert Frost raised an eschatological question: How will the world end? The options he offered were desire (symbolized by fire) or hatred (symbolized by ice). What is not a matter of choice is the fact that the world will one day end.

Eschatology has always been a topic that prophets address. Heaven and hell, although not at the center of daily consciousness for most people, still are with us and will demand our attention. The Advent season provides an opportunity to prepare not only for the Christmas mysteries, but also is an occasion to assess whether or not our lives are moving in the direction of eternal bliss or eternal sadness.

When Jesus was asked about the ministry of Elijah, he informed his disciples that just as Elijah was not recognized by the people of his day, so too the "Son of Man," Jesus himself, would suffer the same fate. And another prophet, John the Baptist, in confronting Herod regarding his adulterous relationship with his brother's wife, would pay the price of execution.

Truth has a price tag. Though truth should lead to freedom, truth that reveals the misconduct of those in authority can lead to violence and death. John the Baptist experienced the hatred that Robert Frost called ice. And Dante, in *The Divine Comedy*, asserted that hell is not fire but a lake of ice.

Sirach writes, "Blessed is he who shall have seen you [Elijah] / and who falls asleep in your friendship" (Sir 48:11). Blessed are all those who fall asleep (die) in the friendship of Jesus and John the Baptist as well.

**Meditation:** What is your understanding of heaven and hell? What do the prophets have to tell us about how we live our lives here and now and how that living shapes our eternal destiny?

**Prayer:** Lord Jesus, draw us up into the mountain of your companionship and teach us how we are to live and how we are to die. Do not let us get caught up in trivialities but help us to see what really matters. May our world not end in ice or hatred, but may it end by your coming in love and peace.

# THIRD WEEK OF ADVENT

# Anointed One: Isaiah, James, John, You and Me

**Readings:** Isa 35:1-6a, 10; Jas 5:7-10; Matt 11:2-11

**Scripture:**
The Spirit of the LORD is upon me,
because he has anointed me
to bring glad tidings to the poor. (Isa 61:1 cited in Luke 4:18)

**Reflection:** The above gospel acclamation is a powerful faith claim, one that all who have been baptized and confirmed can make. The Spirit of the risen Christ is not only upon us but within us. That anointing has within it a mission, that we bring the good news of God's love and mercy, God's glory and splendor, God's compassion and concern to all we meet.

Isaiah was spirit-filled. As a prophet he proclaimed the nearness of God as well as God's marvelous works—the blind will see, the deaf will hear, the lame will walk, the mute will sing. Through grace the blindness of racism is cured, we begin to hear the cry of the poor for the very first time, we leave our comfort zone and walk into the margins of life, we go tell it on the mountains that the Lord of nature and history continues to shape our minds and hearts. Isaiah's strong voice brought confidence and joy to so many over the years.

St. James was anointed with the Spirit of the risen Lord. His message of patience bears much thought and practice.

In a poetic moment, James reminds us that farmers know how to wait and, yes, how to trust. Between planting and harvesting there is an interval over which the farmer has little power. It is the sun and rain, God's creativity made manifest, that bring about growth. Between birth and death there is an interval in which we rely on the grace of light and love to bring us to maturity. Spiritual growth is a gradual and often painful process. The Spirit of patience is necessary if we are to avoid a life of radical frustration.

And then there is John the Baptist, the son of Zechariah and Elizabeth. Early on John experienced the Spirit of God—really early on in the womb. He leapt for joy when the pregnant Mary greeted Elizabeth. Now in prison, John would need the Spirit of faith to sustain him in those dark hours.

The Spirit that we received in baptism and confirmation continues to be operative. Our Advent challenge is to be open and to respond with courage to what God asks of us. We can take consolation in knowing that Isaiah, St. James, and John the Baptist intercede for us and the church this day.

**Meditation:** What do you recall of your confirmation day? What is your relationship with the Holy Spirit? Advocate? Friend? Fire? Love?

**Prayer:** Come, Holy Spirit, enlighten our minds, enkindle our hearts, and empower us to hear God's will and do it. We are often so blind, so deaf, so fearful, so discouraged. Take away our fear and give us the grace to become good disciples and stewards. Come, Holy Spirit, come.

*December 12:*
*Our Lady of Guadalupe* (Catholic Church)
*Monday of the Third Week of Advent*
(Episcopal Church)

## Invasions of Grace

**Readings:** Zech 2:14-17 or Rev 11:19a; 12:1-6a; Luke 1:39-47 or Luke 1:26-38

**Scripture:**
The angel Gabriel was sent from God
  to a town of Galilee called Nazareth,
  to a virgin betrothed to a man named Joseph,
  of the house of David,
  and the virgin's name was Mary. (Luke 1:26)

**Reflection:** Many individuals who have traveled to Lourdes or Fatima or Guadalupe came home changed. These sites have special meaning for people of faith; these sites offer many graces, be the grace one of reconciliation, healing, or a deepening of compassion. These Marian apparitions have transformed not only individuals, but nations as well.

I once heard a theologian talk about "the invasions of grace." God, like the lion Aslan in C. S. Lewis's *Chronicles of Narnia*, is on the move. God sends messengers: Gabriel to the town of Nazareth; dreams to Joseph in Egypt; Raphael to Tobiah. God sends messengers into our lives through an elementary schoolteacher, a friend who takes us to task, a sudden illness, or a surprised success. God is on the move; Love, God's proper name, is always active.

It was December 9, 1531, when Juan Diego, a Christian Indian living near the present-day Mexico City, felt the invasion of grace. He experienced an apparition of Mary. The rest of the story is quite familiar: a shrine was built at the site; a people felt the compassion of God; the call to serve the poor was given.

Mary's life focused on doing God's will. From her place in heaven, Mary continues to be an instrument of God's will. She intercedes for all of God's children, praying that we be open to the invasions of God's grace, the grace of God's love and mercy.

**Meditation:** Where have you seen the invasions (apparitions) of God's grace? In what ways can you be an agent of God's love and mercy in our world?

**Prayer:** Mary, Our Lady of Guadalupe, pray for us. Help us to build the church, to encourage and affirm one another in the doing of God's will. Deepen our faith; expand our hope; strengthen our charity.

*December 13:*
*Saint Lucy, Virgin and Martyr* (Catholic Church)

*Tuesday of the Third Week of Advent*
(Episcopal Church)

## Case Studies

**Readings:** Zeph 3:1-2, 9-13; Matt 21:28-32

**Scripture:**
Jesus said . . .
"What is your opinion?
A man had two sons." (Matt 21:28a)

**Reflection:** Jesus loved to teach by way of parables. In the story of the prodigal son, Jesus tells of a man who had two sons. The younger son squanders his inheritance while the elder son remains faithful to his duties. One does the father's will, the other does not. Again in today's gospel, we are given a similar starting point but a different conclusion. The two sons here have to decide whether they do what the father requests or not. The theme is the same in both situations: doing or not doing the Father's will.

We have another case study of obedience in the life of Jesus' mother. Mary, our model and mentor for Advent, not only does God's will, but she encourages others to be obedient as well. In the miracle at Cana, she tells the servants *to* "*do* whatever he [Jesus] tells you." They did her bidding and the bidding of her son. Water becomes wine and the wedding

 *Third Week of Advent*

celebration continues. Obedience leads to joy no matter how difficult God's demands are.

And how about this case study? Mother Teresa of Calcutta struggled to know what God was asking of her. Through prayer and counsel, she came to the conclusion that God was asking her to leave the religious community she loved and to start a new ministry to the poorest of the poor. Her example demonstrates the power of obedience.

And our case study? We too are asked to do God's will as the prophet Micah presents it: act justly, love tenderly, and live in faith (6:8). Nothing more is asked of us . . . and nothing less.

**Meditation:** What is God asking of you during this Advent season? To visit a homebound person? To refrain from gossiping? To celebrate the sacrament of reconciliation?

**Prayer:** Lord Jesus, in the Garden of Gethsemane, you once again embraced your Father's will. Help us to be obedient and to do with joy what you ask of us. Send your Spirit of courage into our lives so that the work of justice and peace might be done. Come, Lord Jesus, come.

*December 14:*
*Saint John of the Cross* (Catholic Church)

*Wednesday of the Third Week of Advent*
(Episcopal Church)

## Stumbling Block/Absurdity

**Readings:** Isa 45:6c-8, 18, 21b-25; Luke 7:18b-23

**Scripture:**
"And blessed is the one who takes no offense at me."
   (Luke 7:23)

**Reflection:** In writing to the Corinthians (1 Cor 1:23), St. Paul had to deal with how Jesus was perceived. For the Jews, the crucified Christ was a stumbling block; for the Gentiles, Christ crucified was an absurdity. No wonder St. Paul struggled in his mission of evangelization.

Looking back at the presentation of the child Jesus in the temple, Simon tells Mary that her child will be a sign of contradiction, indeed, the very downfall and rise of many (Luke 2:34). Both at birth and at death, the Advent Jesus challenged the understanding of almost everyone. Bethlehem and Calvary would be hard to fathom.

Stumbling block! As we travel life's journey there will be obstacles at every level: physical, emotional, social, and intellectual. And, yes, in our faith. Are we really expected to believe in the virgin birth, or the miracles that Jesus performed, or the mystery of the resurrection? Narrow rationalism is totally befuddled.

Absurdity! Is it not sheer foolishness to claim that God would become one of us in Christ? And then the scandal of particularity that theologians talk about—that in this place, at this time, in a small hamlet, the Savior of the world is born and lived and died and rose from the dead! Without faith, how can this make sense or provide meaning?

St. Paul had faith; Simeon and Mary had faith; millions upon millions of people down the ages had faith. Jesus was not a stumbling block or an absurdity. He was the Light of the World, the very enfleshment of God, our savior and re-deemer and friend.

**Meditation:** Do you have to deal with stumbling blocks as you attempt to accept and live the gift of faith? Does absurdity ever plague your mind and soul?

**Prayer:** Crucified and risen Lord, we beg for a deep and abiding faith. May we come to know and love you in new and profound ways. May we participate in your life now so that we might share in the glory of your resurrection.

## Good, Better, Great!

**Readings:** Isa 54:1-10; Luke 7:24-30

**Scripture:**
"I tell you,
   among those born of women, no one is greater than John;
   yet the least in the Kingdom of God is greater than he."
      (Luke 7:28)

**Reflection:** Jesus had great admiration for John the Baptist. Here was a prophet of great courage, asceticism, and commitment. The Baptist's life was consumed by the mystery of God. And yet Jesus makes what seems a strange statement, namely, that anyone (and there must be millions of saints) in God's kingdom is greater than John.

I will leave this dilemma to the Scripture scholars. What we should try to figure out is what makes John the Baptist so great. We know from Jesus' teaching that the most important thing is that all of life is love, the litmus test of discipleship and greatness. Unless we love, we miss out on the meaning of life.

So, what is love? Is love the experience of one's puzzling solidarity with our neighbors and strangers? When the Trappist Thomas Merton stood on a street corner in Louisville, Kentucky, and felt a oneness with all the anonymous people at that intersection, it was love that coursed through his being. John the Baptist knew his oneness with all humanity.

Is love the phenomenon of care, the concern that the Good Samaritan had for the person who was beaten and robbed at the roadside? More, love is not just an internal care but a grace that expresses itself in active assistance to others. John the Baptist knew such care and compassion.

**Meditation:** What is your understanding of greatness? Who are the people in history or in your personal life whom you would call great? Are there any "days" in the past month that you would call great?

**Prayer:** Lord Jesus, teach us to experience and understand your love for us. Teach us to share that love with others so that we might merit a portion of John the Baptist's greatness. Send the Spirit of compassion and solidarity into our lives.

## Yves Congar: An Advent Person

**Readings:** Isa 56:1-3a, 6-8; John 5:33-36

**Scripture:**
For my house shall be called
  a house of prayer for all peoples.
Thus says the Lord GOD,
  who gathers the dispersed of Israel:
Others will I gather to him
  besides those already gathered. (Isa 56:7c-8)

**Reflection:** One of the greatest theologians of the twentieth century was the Dominican scholar Yves Congar (1904–95). He had a passion for ecumenism and his writings and teaching influenced not only the Vatican II document *Unitatis Redintegratio*, the Decree on Ecumenism, but also the documents on revelation and the church.

Congar could identify with Isaiah's verse that God's house of prayer is indeed for all peoples. This Dominican priest fought long and hard to overcome the divisions in the Body of Christ and strove to show how God's truth, beauty, and goodness was contained in all authentic religious traditions. He called for an openness to finding truth wherever God had planted it.

In the gospel today Jesus reminds us that he was sent by the Father for the salvation of the world. Jesus came so that all might be one, that all might be reconciled to the Father and to one another. Yves Congar put all his energy into fostering that unity and reconciliation. In spite of harsh criticism and being silenced, he continued to seek the unity Christ so desired.

As we approach the Christmas mystery, we see in the magi those outside the Jewish tradition who came to encounter the person of Jesus. Everyone is called to that encounter and Congar's mission was to facilitate that meeting.

**Meditation:** What has been your experience of other Christian traditions and other world religions? What truth and goodness have you experienced from them?

**Prayer:** Lord Jesus, you prayed that all might be one. Give us the courage to end division and be reconciled to one another and to all we meet. May the Spirit of unity reign in our hearts and in our institutions. Come, Lord Jesus, come.

## Hodgepodge

**Readings:** Gen 49:2, 8-10; Matt 1:1-17

**Scripture:**
The book of the genealogy of Jesus Christ,
   the son of David, the son of Abraham. (Matt 1:1)

**Reflection:** Right off the bat, in the very first chapter, the very first verse of Matthew's gospel, we are made aware of Jesus' identification with our humanity. He came and took on our flesh so that we might share in his divinity: "By the mystery of this water and wine / may we come to share in the divinity of Christ / who humbled himself to share in our humanity" (offertory prayer).

Carefully note the first two names in Jesus' genealogy: Abraham and David. Abraham was dishonest at times; David was immoral (murder and adultery). These were Jesus' ancestors; these are our ancestors in faith. Through the mystery of the incarnation Jesus humbled himself, emptied himself so that we might realize how much he loves us and how deeply he understands our human plight.

The expression "hodgepodge" refers to a disordered, confused situation. The history that Jesus entered was a mess and a jumble, and yet he came. Saint Paul makes this abundantly clear when he tells us that even while we (Abraham,

David, you and I) were still sinners, the Lord came to rescue us from our sins and our fears (Rom 5:8).

The great theologian Karl Rahner was not afraid to ask the big questions: "Why is world history a single stream of stupidity, crudity, and brutality?" His language is stronger than "hodgepodge," but it makes the same point: our world is a mess and Jesus plunged into it to be with us and take us home.

**Meditation:** What has been your experience of history—kind or cruel? What legacy have you been given through genealogy?

**Prayer:** Jesus, the wisdom and power of God, we give you thanks for coming into our messy world. May we truly share in your divinity as you have shared in our humanity. Empty us of selfishness; give us your wisdom and the grace of prudence.

# FOURTH WEEK OF ADVENT

## The Obedience of Faith

**Readings:** Isa 7:10-14; Rom 1:1-7; Matt 1:18-24

**Scripture:**
Through him [Jesus] we have received the grace of
   apostleship,
   to bring about the obedience of faith,
   for the sake of his name, among all the Gentiles . . .
      (Rom 1:5a)

**Reflection:** What a grace it is to be clear about one's mission. Saint Paul's clarity about his being chosen "to bring about the obedience of faith" and to know the people to whom he was sent to achieve this work is truly a blessing. Many of us never achieve that certitude and, because of the lack of clarity, precious energy is lost.

It wasn't always that obvious to Paul what his mission in life was. His initial mistake in persecuting the early Christian community would find him cast to the ground and experiencing blindness. We know the story; we know how Jesus broke into Paul's life and graced him with an apostleship that helped shaped the Christian world. It was about faith in Christ; it was all about being obedient to the Spirit of the risen Christ.

Like Paul, Joseph was a man of faith and obedience. Though Joseph did not comprehend all that had happened to Mary, he did believe the message of the angel and then, in supreme obedience, did what was asked of him. The obedience of faith is at the heart of discipleship as is witnessed in Mary, Joseph, and Paul, as is manifest in the lives of all saints.

There is no room for romanticism when it comes to faith or obedience. The Southern Catholic writer Flannery O'Connor, detesting sentimentality, asserts that faith is about the cross and is not one big electric blanket. Though Bethlehem is close at hand, there is always the shadow of the cross that we have to deal with. Faith is costly and Joseph, Mary, and Paul paid the price, the giving of their wills over to God's design.

A word about Ahaz. He is one of us. We all look for assurance and a sign would be very helpful to firm up our belief. Blind faith, like blind obedience, demands extreme trust in God's providential care. May we be granted that confidence in this Advent season and throughout our lives.

**Meditation:** What do you understand by the phrase "the obedience of faith"? Who are the people in your life who have demonstrated radical faith and joyful obedience? Which of the components of faith—conviction, confidence, commitment—is most difficult for you?

**Prayer:** Lord Jesus, you were obedient to what the Father asked, obedient even unto death. Draw us more deeply into the mystery of discipleship. Help us to believe and to do what the Father asks of us. And when we fail, do not let us become discouraged. Come, Lord Jesus, come.

*December 19: Monday of the Fourth Week of Advent*

## Prayers: Answered and Unanswered

**Readings:** Judg 13:2-7, 24-25a; Luke 1:5-25

**Scripture:**
But the angel said to him, "Do not be afraid, Zechariah,
    because your prayer has been heard.
Your wife Elizabeth will bear you a son,
    and you shall name him John." (Luke 1:13)

**Reflection:** At the start of Lent, the three large imperatives are direct and clear: pray, fast, give alms. During the season of Advent, those same imperatives apply as we grow in our relationship with God by way of mutual communication, as we strive to get our own lives in order through the disciplines of fasting and self-denial, as we reach out to our sisters and brothers in need.

Zechariah was a man of prayer. He desperately wanted a family, but Elizabeth was old and barren. Zechariah did not give up hope. His prayer for a child was answered and his "disgrace before others" was taken away.

Not all prayers are answered, at least in terms of what one may be asking for. The sick, for whom we pray to get well, often die; the barren woman desiring to give birth to a child remains barren, her pleas apparently unheeded; petitions for the end of war seem to have no effect. We may be tempted to file these prayers as "unanswered."

A mature spirituality has more subtlety than the categories of answered and unanswered prayers. True disciples have a radical, fundamental prayer: "Thy will be done!" The question is not fertility or barrenness, not sickness or health, not success or failure. The question is the realization of God's will. God's perspective transcends our limited comprehension because God knows what is best for us. "Unanswered prayers" are sometimes our greatest blessings.

**Meditation:** What role does prayer play in your life? Fasting? Almsgiving? What is your understanding of praying that God's will be done, not your own?

**Prayer:** Loving God, help us to pray. Teach us the mystery of your divine providence and enable us to be obedient to your slight stirring within. May we not focus on our needs or wants, but on what leads to justice and peace, qualities of your kingdom.

## Where Do You Dwell?

**Readings:** Isa 7:10-14; Luke 1:26-38

**Scripture:**
"And behold, Elizabeth, your relative,
   has also conceived a son in her old age,
   and this is the sixth month for her who was called
      barren;
   for nothing will be impossible for God." (Luke 1:36-37)

**Reflection:** The famous New England poet Emily Dickinson began one of her verses with these words: "I dwell in Possibility." The famous maiden from Nazareth, Mary, the mother of Jesus, could have said, "I dwell in Impossibilities!" For how could she, not having relations with a man, be pregnant? How could her cousin Elizabeth, far beyond childbearing age, have a child in her womb? Impossible?

But the angel Gabriel, knowing the mystery and power of God, exclaims, "for nothing will be impossible for God." How is it that death yields to resurrection, or that sin can be forgiven, or hatred will be conquered by love? When the Holy Spirit comes upon the world everything changes.

Ms. Dickinson speaks about dwelling in "Possibility." Yet even though a questionable believer, the poet wrote that people who loved or who were loved could not die. Why? Because love is immortal. Her skeptical friends might have told her that this is impossible.

Mary was loved by God and she in turn loved her Creator. How else can we comprehend how she could utter those glorious words: "Behold, I am the handmaid of the Lord. May it be done to me according to your word" (Luke 1:38)?

**Meditation:** Do you dwell in the land of possibilities or impossibilities? Have any angels (teachers, wisdom figures, mentors) ever appeared to you with a message from God?

**Prayer:** Mary, faith-filled and obedient servant of the Lord, intercede for us. May we come to appreciate more deeply the workings of God in our personal lives and in history. May we, like you, hear God's voice and do what he asks of us.

*December 21: Wednesday of the Fourth Week of Advent*

## The Passing of Winter

**Readings:** Song 2:8-14 or Zeph 3:14-18a; Luke 1:39-45

**Scripture:**
My lover speaks; he says to me,
   "Arise, my beloved, my dove, my beautiful one,
   and come!
"For see, the winter is past,
   the rains are over and gone.
The flowers appear on the earth . . ." (Song 2:10-12a)

**Reflection:** For those who live in a wintery world, with ice and snow, with darkness and frigid temperatures, what glory when spring arrives with its flowers and warmth, its light and newness. New life is in the land with fig trees producing their fruit, vine branches blooming, and sweet aroma filling the air.

At times winter comes upon human relationships. Whatever the cause, be it loneliness or separation or lostness, what joy when someone who loves us approaches. Suddenly, our hearts expand and a sense of well-being sweeps through the soul. In faith, we believe that God, whose proper name is Love, comes like the spring into our lives whenever we open ourselves to grace. God is the Lover who sees us as beautiful and, as the poet Gerard Manley Hopkins says, "worthy the winning."

In Mary's visitation of Elizabeth what mutual affection we see. These two pregnant women, both attempting to deal with the mysterious workings of grace, sensed that the winter of confusion and barrenness was coming to an end. Love filled the air in their exchange with one another; Love filled their wombs with light and new life.

In his *On-Going Incarnation: Johann Adam Mohler and the Beginning of Modern Eccelesiology*, the theologian Michael Himes writes about faith as flowing from the experience of "being grasped by God." It is in that experience of being embraced and loved by God that the winter of doubt is over and spring has come.

**Meditation:** What is your experience of being grasped by God, being taken by the hand? Does the soul have its seasons—spring, summer, autumn, and winter?

**Prayer:** Gracious and loving God, help us to experience you taking us by the hand. Drive the winter out of our lives; gift us with spring and new life. Then we will be able to give life to others and help them experience the warmth of your abiding love.

## Emancipation: The Grace of Freedom

**Readings:** 1 Sam 1:24-28; Luke 1:46-56

**Scripture:**
Mary said:
"My soul proclaims the greatness of the Lord;
my spirit rejoices in God my savior,
for he has looked upon his lowly servant."
(Luke 1:46-48a)

**Reflection:** On January 1, 1863, President Abraham Lincoln issued the Emancipation Proclamation, an executive order declaring freedom to those held in the bondage of slavery. One can only imagine the rejoicing of those freed from the brutality of slavery. Lincoln would go down in history as a courageous and great leader.

Mary, in her song of praise, sung of another emancipation. For Mary, God was Lord and Savior. In her son Jesus, people would be set free from the slavery of sin and death. Mary went on to sing of God's love, his strength and might, his concern for the hungry and the lowly, his promise of mercy. Mary knew firsthand the greatness of God.

Not only is Mary's song one of praise, but it is also a song of tremendous joy. Mary *rejoices*; she celebrates deep in her soul that fundamental graced experience of being looked on with love. Herein is the source of happiness and peace;

herein is cause of joy and serenity. And the love that she received, Mary would pass on to all she would meet.

Not everyone appreciated President Lincoln's Emancipation Proclamation. Not everyone appreciates Mary's proclamation of God's greatness. Because of tragedies in life, incredible suffering, or personal sins, God is experienced as uncaring or God's very existence is denied. Many individuals have never felt that they have been looked at in a loving fashion. For them Mary prays; for all of us Mary prays that we might experience the greatness of a loving, merciful God revealed in Jesus.

**Meditation:** In what does "greatness" consist? Is it possible to be loved and not sing? In what ways has God freed you?

**Prayer:** Mary, pray that we might know God's greatness revealed in Jesus. Intercede for our world that deals with slavery in so many forms. May we be free like you to proclaim the wonder of God's love and mercy. And, yes, pray for us at the hour of our death.

## Heartfelt Singing and Living

**Readings:** Mal 3:1-4, 23-24; Luke 1:57-66

**Scripture:**
All who heard these things took them to heart, saying,
  "What, then, will this child be?
For surely the hand of the Lord was with him." (Luke 1:66)

**Reflection:** Hesychius, an early church writer, urges his readers to sing in this fashion: "Let mind and heart be in your song: this is to glorify God with your whole self" (Divine Office, Sunday, Week IV).

We read in today's gospel that the friends of Elizabeth and Zechariah took to heart the events surrounding John's birth. Taking things to heart, be those things a poem or a psalm or a melody, transforms our interior terrain. Too often our minds and hearts are not engaged in the event before us. Like water off a duck's back, experiences come and go without much effect.

As Christmas approaches in just two days, we want to be attentive to the messengers that God sends us and we want to allow our hearts to be open to God's daily graces. The prophet Malachi tells how God will send Elijah "[t]o turn the hearts of the fathers to their children, / and the hearts of the children to their fathers" (Mal 3:24). Zechariah, in the naming of John, turned his heart to his newborn son. The father knew that the hand of the Lord rested upon him. And the son, John the Baptist, would turn his heart to the heavenly Father and do God's will.

As we sing our Advent and Christmas hymns, songs that carry our theology, let our hearts be in those songs. If so, we give glory to God because we are living life to the full. Surely the songs that John sang were the psalms; surely those psalms, when sung, came from his heart.

**Meditation:** Is your heart in the songs you sing, in the experiences of the day? Why is it difficult to keep our minds focused and our hearts engaged?

**Prayer:** Lord Jesus, you call us to live life, life to the full. Grace us with attentiveness of mind and openness of heart. May we glorify you and your Father by taking your love and mercy to heart. May we then share that mercy and love with all we meet.

## *In Umbra Mortis*
## (In the Shadow of Death)

**Readings:** 2 Sam 7:1-5, 8b-12, 14a, 16; Luke 1:67-79

**Scripture:**
"In the tender compassion of our God
    the dawn from on high shall break upon us,
    to shine on those who dwell in darkness and the
        shadow of death,
    and to guide our feet into the way of peace."
    (Luke 1:78-79)

**Reflection:**
    In Umbra Mortis

    Here we sit,
        billions of us on our small planet,
        using artificial light to scatter the ubiquitous
            darkness,
        running here and there and everywhere
        to distract us from impending death.

    Here we sit,
        looking to the east,
        hoping beyond hope that the Light will come,
        justice too—and truth and charity.

Here we sit,
  chanting our humble antiphons
  convinced that God's glory is near,
  is here in Jesus.

No longer does darkness reign,
no longer does death terrify.

The Dayspring has sprung,
the shadowland is no more.

**Meditation:** How do you deal with the mystery of death? Denial or acceptance?

**Prayer:** Jesus, you are the Sun of justice, the Light of the World, our morning Star. You come to break the bonds of death, to take us out of the shadowland into the fullness of life. Deepen our faith in the mystery of the resurrection.

# SEASON OF CHRISTMAS

*December 25: The Nativity of the Lord* (Christmas)

## Now/Today—At This Present Time

**Readings:**
*VIGIL:* Isa 62:1-5; Acts 13:16-17, 22-25; Matt 1:1-25
  (or 1:18-25)
*NIGHT:* Isa 9:1-6; Titus 2:11-14; Luke 2:1-14
*DAWN:* Isa 62:11-12; Titus 3:4-7; Luke 2:15-20
*DAY:* Isa 52:7-10; Heb 1:1-6; John 1:1-18 (or 1:1-5, 9-14)

**Scripture:**
"For today in the city of David
  a savior has been born for you who is Christ and Lord."
    (Luke 2:11)

**Reflection:** The German theologian Gerhard Lohfink in his
books on Christology (*Jesus of Nazareth* and *No Irrelevant
Jesus*) emphasizes time and time again the concept of "today."
For Lohfink, the preaching and practice of Jesus is this
"now," this "today," that gives the gospels such urgency. The
kingdom of God is now; repent and believe today; salvation
is taking place right under our nose.

As we celebrate the nativity of our Lord we might ask how,
in this moment, is Christ being born within us and our
world? If Gerhard Lohfink is correct, is the birth of Jesus
happening now, today?

In our hymn "Good Christian Men, Rejoice" we sing:
"Good Christian men, rejoice / with heart and soul and

voice; / give ye heed to what we say: / Jesus Christ was born today. / Ox and ass before him bow / And he is in the manger now. / Christ is born today! / Christ is born today!" *Now! Today!*

When nations cease their wars and live in peace, when life is chosen over death, when love governs our hearts and our families, when justice is done to one and all, when truth is told and deceptions end, when freedom conquers slavery, when . . . In these moments and in whatever place, Christ is born and we rejoice.

**Meditation:** In what sense is the birth of Christ happening in our time, in our space? Is being truly "present" to one another and to our God perhaps the best Christmas present ever?

**Prayer:** Lord Jesus, son of God and son of Mary, deepen our faith to see your life-giving grace all over the place. May we have a sense of urgency that today, right now we are in the midst of your loving revelation. With heart, soul, and voice, may we rejoice.

## *In Manus Tuas* (Into Your Hands)

**Readings:** Acts 6:8-10; 7:54-59; Matt 10:17-22

**Scripture:**
As they were stoning Stephen, he called out
  "Lord Jesus, receive my spirit." (Acts 7:59)

**Reflection:** The psalmist cried out, "Into your hands I commend my spirit; / you will redeem me, O LORD, O faithful God" (Ps 31:6). Jesus from the cross uttered a loud cry: "Father, into your hands I commend my spirit" (Luke 23:46). And Stephen, while being stoned, prayed, "Lord Jesus, receive my spirit" (Acts 7:59b).

In between our birth and our death, we all live active lives. We grow up, go to school, make decisions about work, develop relationships, and exercise our freedom on many fronts. We were not in control when we were born. But when the hour of our death comes, we may or may not be able to make choices. The psalmist, Jesus, and Stephen faced the mystery of death with a prayer, a prayer commending their life and last breath to the Father.

Stephen was stoned to death. Jesus was crucified. We don't know how the psalmist died. Whether death comes through violence or from old age, we do pass into the mystery of eternity. Faith promises us a homecoming and fills the soul with hope. For the nonbeliever, death may be a passing into nothingness since there is nothing beyond the limits of time and space. If death claims finality, despair can sweep through the soul.

Stephen was a man of faith and hope. He believed in Jesus and the Lord's promise of eternal life. For Stephen, death was not an end of existence but a passage into eternal life. The moment of his death turned into a homecoming and his spirit was received by the Lord Jesus.

**Meditation:** What is your experience of death in your family and social circle? What attitude might we pray for in our daily dying to selfishness?

**Prayer:** St. Stephen, intercede for us, especially when we deal with the mystery of death. Pray that we may commend our spirit to a living, forgiving God; pray that we may be free from despair and resentment in our final hours.

## Joyful Messengers

**Readings:** 1 John 1:1-4; John 20:1a, 2-8

**Scripture:**
. . . what we have seen and heard
we proclaim now to you,
so that you too may have fellowship with us;
for our fellowship is with the Father
and with his Son, Jesus Christ. (1 John 1:3)

**Reflection:** In writing about the church's ministry of evangelization, Pope Francis states with great force in his apostolic exhortation *Evangelii Gaudium*, "Rather than experts in dire predictions, dour judges bent on rooting out every threat and deviation, we should appear as joyful messengers of challenging proposals, guardians of the goodness and beauty which shine forth in a life of fidelity to the Gospel" (168). To drive home the point about being joyful messengers, he writes, "an evangelizer must never look like someone who has just come back from a funeral" (5).

The core message of Christianity is God's love and mercy that comes to us through the person of Jesus, crucified and risen. The source of joy is God's love; the source of peace is God's mercy. We have good news to communicate to a world that deals with so much darkness, despair, and death. Our daily papers and news reports narrate what we see and hear in our war-torn countries and broken institutions and relationships. But there is other news, the news that arises from the mystery of the resurrection, the news that love and life are stronger than death.

The joy that filled the hearts of Mary, Peter, and John had to be shared. Jesus, tortured and killed, is alive. God's mercy and love is offered to us day in and day out as we celebrate the paschal mystery. To be complete, joy must be shared.

**Meditation:** Do you see yourself as an evangelist? How can you share the good news of the Gospel with your family, friends, and coworkers?

**Prayer:** Spirit of the risen Lord, fill us with an active joy that compels us to go forth and proclaim the Father's love and mercy. Take away our hesitancy; give us the courage to witness to the good news. Come, Holy Spirit, come.

*December 28: The Holy Innocents, Martyrs*

## Light and Darkness; Hope and Despair

**Readings:** 1 John 1:5–2:2; Matt 2:13-18

**Scripture:**
When Herod realized that he had been deceived by the
    magi,
  he became furious. (Matt 2:13a)

**Reflection:** Herod walked in darkness. It was the darkness
of anger that led to violence and the massacre of small children. His rage destroyed innocent life; his fear was the loss
of power.

Jesus came to bring us light and life. His plunge into history was a plunge into violence and terror. He embraced our
human condition and would one day suffer crucifixion. The
children of Bethlehem died young; Jesus would die on the
cross some years later, a victim of religious and political
power.

This feast of the Holy Innocents brings us face-to-face with
the dark side of history. There is a danger of being over-
whelmed by ethnic cleansings and civil wars, by corrupt
leaders in every segment of society, by the bullying and cru-
elty of even the young. Pessimism can sweep through the
human heart.

We need the grace of faith and hope on our human journey.
The God who created us not only continues to sustain us but

has come to live among us. God still abides in the sacraments, in the Scriptures and community, in the depth of our hearts. Saint John reminds us that the Blood of Jesus cleanses us of our sin, reconciliation is possible, and peace can be achieved.

Our Emeritus Pope Benedict XVI speaks about hope: "The dark door of time, of the future, has been thrown open. The one who has hope lives differently; the one who hopes has been granted the gift of a new life" (*Spe Salvi* 2). Because of the nativity of our Lord, we have hope, a hope that confirms that the Holy Innocents share in God's glory.

**Meditation:** Does too much reading of history or current events threaten your hope? What are some ways of sustaining hope in a world wrestling with so much darkness?

**Prayer:** God of light, we give you thanks for sending us your Son Jesus to enlighten us on our journey. Sometimes the darkness is overwhelming; sometimes our hope is threatened. Deepen our trust in you and help us to be agents of your light and love.

*December 29:*
*Saint Thomas Becket, Bishop and Martyr*
(Catholic Church, optional memorial)

*Fifth Day in the Octave of Christmas*
(Episcopal Church)

## Love's Synonym: For

**Readings:** 1 John 2:3-11; Luke 2:22-35

**Scripture:**
Beloved:
The way we may be sure that we know Jesus
    is to keep his commandments. (1 John 2:3)

**Reflection:** In Shakespeare's *King Lear*, Lear's daughter
Regan arrogantly says of her father, "'Tis the infirmity of his
age; yet he hath ever but slenderly known himself" (I.i.293).
Self-knowledge is difficult; knowledge of who Jesus is also
has its challenges.

In the above Scripture passage St. John lays it on the line:
the only certainty we have that we know who Jesus is comes
from keeping his commandments, the love of God and the
love of our neighbor. It is not in study that we attain this
knowledge; it is in the *doing* of God's will. God is Love and
only "lovers," people who are for others, will come to understand some dimension of the mystery of God.

Thomas Becket (1118–70), chancellor of King Henry II and
archbishop of Canterbury, was slain at the altar for opposing

the king's policies regarding the church's independence. Becket, through fasting and prayer, began to have knowledge of Jesus and what his office as bishop meant. He, Becket, was to be *for* the people, *for* the church, *for* the doing of God's will. The word *for* is another name for love.

In the presentation mystery we hear of the elderly Simeon now ready to die. Simeon saw in Mary's child someone "destined for the fall and rise of many in Israel" (Luke 2:34b). This child was "for" others in this purification rite and in his living and dying. Here was the light to the nations; here was the glory of Israel.

The American essayist Ralph Waldo Emerson stated, "Only so much do I know, as I have lived" ("The American Scholar," 1837). Sure knowledge comes from doing. It is in keeping the commandments that we have knowledge of Jesus. Our Christology depends upon loving, upon being for others.

**Meditation:** What do you know about yourself, about Jesus? How did you arrive at this knowledge? Is the word "for" just another word for love?

**Prayer:** Lord God, your commandments are clear and direct. Send your Spirit upon us, as you did upon Simeon, that we might come to know you more deeply. May we be for others as you are for us.

*December 30:*
*The Holy Family of Jesus, Mary and Joseph*
(Catholic Church)

*Sixth Day in the Octave of Christmas*
(Episcopal Church)

## Holy Family: A Feast of Gratitude

**Readings:** Sir 3:2-6, 12-14 or Col 3:12-21 or 3:12-17;
Matt 2:13-15, 19-23

**Scripture:**
Put on, as God's chosen ones, holy and beloved,
  heartfelt compassion, kindness, humility, gentleness,
    and patience,
  bearing with one another and forgiving one another . . .
  as the Lord has forgiven you, so must you also do.
    (Col 3:12-13)

**Reflection:** St. Paul understood well the qualities of graced relationships: compassion, kindness, humility, gentleness, patience, and forgiveness. A few verses later he adds yet another virtue that provides a solid pillar of strong family life: gratitude—we are always to be thankful.

In his powerful poem "Those Winter Sundays," Robert Hayden describes a father who serves his family so well: driving out the coldness of winter, polishing shoes, working hard to provide for his family. The poem contains a brief, five-word sentence that is devastating: "No one ever thanked him."

On this feast of the Holy Family, we might examine the quality of our gratitude. Do we as a family of humankind thank God our Father for all that has been given to us? Our providential God has given us the gift of life (creation), the gift of salvation (redemption), the gift of the Spirit (sanctification). Day in and day out we are a blessed family, surrounded by God's grace and love. Is a refrain echoing over the corridors of history: "No one ever thanked him"?

No mention is made in the gospels as to Mary's gratitude for all that Joseph did for her and Jesus. But we can be assured that she was thankful. Mary knew and proclaimed in the *Magnificat* the great things God had done for her; Mary surely sang the praises of Joseph as well. And add to this Mary's compassion and kindness, humility and gentleness, patience and forgiveness, and you have the workings of a good family.

In Flannery O'Connor's short story "Greenleaf," we read: "Some people learn gratitude too late, Mr. Greenleaf, and some never learn it at all." Those two little words—"thank you"— should be forever on our lips as we ponder the many blessings that have come our way from God, family, and friends.

**Meditation:** How do you express your gratitude to God and family? How do you react when you gift people and there is no response?

**Prayer:** Generous God, give us grateful hearts. May we never take you or our family for granted. As we retire to bed every night, may we count our blessings instead of sheep. Then we will experience your joy and peace.

## Oplatki: Breaking Bread Together

**Readings:** 1 John 2:18-21; John 1:1-18

**Scripture:**
In the beginning was the Word,
  and the Word was with God,
  and the Word was God.
He was in the beginning with God. (John 1:1-2)

**Reflection:** Oplatki are unleavened wafers that resemble the communion wafers used at Mass. It is Polish custom that on Christmas Eve, as families gather around the table, the father or eldest member of the household breaks off a piece of the wafer and then passes it around to each member at the table. Prayers are said to give thanks for the blessings of the year or to ask for forgiveness and reconciliation. This ancient Polish custom fosters unity and a sense of peace.

On this last day of the year, we look back on the gift of 365 days. We do well to give thanks and ask forgiveness; we do well to foster the unity of our families and of our world. Jesus, the Word made flesh, came into the world to save us from sin and to break the bonds of death. This Jesus, the eternal Word, reveals to us the mystery of Divinity. John the Baptist testified to the Father's only-begotten Son, and when Jesus came, John's work was done.

When we gather around our family table or the eucharistic altar, listening to the word of God and breaking bread, we celebrate the call to community, to be the Body of Christ. When we celebrate well, we experience the grace and truth that comes to us through Jesus Christ. In that communion the glory of God is made manifest and joy and peace enter our hearts.

On this eve of a new year, we do well to ponder how God's grace impacted our lives over the past twelve months. And in that pondering, let us give thanks for the life-giving moments of grace; let us ask pardon for our sins of commission and omission.

**Meditation:** What family customs do you have that foster God's grace of unity and peace? As the New Year approaches, how can you be a source of grace to others?

**Prayer:** Jesus, Word made flesh, we give you thanks for dwelling among us and taking to yourself our human condition. Help us to be thankful for all your gifts; help us to repent of deeds done and not done. May we live in your grace and truth in the New Year.

*January 1:*
*Solemnity of Mary, Mother of God* (Catholic Church)
*Holy Name of Jesus* (Episcopal Church)

## *Ave Maria!*

**Readings:** Num 6:22-27; Gal 4:4-7; Luke 2:16-21

**Scripture:**
The shepherds went in haste to Bethlehem and found
    Mary and Joseph,
  and the infant lying in the manger. (Luke 2:16)

**Reflection:** Often at wedding and funerals, Franz Schubert's *Ave Maria* is sung. Several passages of that beautiful hymn and prayer merit pondering in our hearts, just as Mary reflected upon the amazing message she heard from the shepherds in Bethlehem.

*Gratia plena!* Mary is one full of grace, favored in a unique way by God in her participation in the mystery of our redemption. The grace that filled her being was that of life, love, and light. The Lord of all life was with her, dwelling within in her womb; the Spirit of love radiated from her reflective and tender heart; the light of God's glory shone in her words and very presence. The grace that she received she gave to all whom she encountered.

*Mater Dei!* Mary is proclaimed the mother of God for she bore the Christ who was human and divine. As the mother of Jesus, she became the mother and model for the church.

A good mother is one who listens and loves. Mary was obedient to the word she heard from God; Mary was responsive in her active concern for all she met. Mary's obedience and self-giving mirrors our eucharistic celebration.

*Ora pro nobis peccatoribus*! We ask Mary to pray for all of us, we who are sinners and in need of redemption. That prayer is not only when we face the mystery of death, but in our everyday life as we struggle to be free from sin and faithful disciples of the Lord. Our pilgrimage is long and difficult. We need much grace to be true to our baptismal commitments.

**Meditation:** What role does the "Hail Mary" play in your spiritual life? What phrases in the prayer are most meaningful to you?

**Prayer:** Mary, Mother of God, continue to pray for us. You experienced our human condition of not knowing what the future held; you had to deal with fear. Help us to be open to God's many graces. May we emulate you in being obedient and self-giving.

*January 2:*
*Saints Basil the Great and Gregory Nazianzen, Bishops*
*and Doctors of the Church* (Catholic Church)

## Finding Our Voice

**Readings:** 1 John 2:22-28; John 1:19-28

**Scripture:**
He [John] said:
> "I am *the voice of one crying out in the desert,*
> *'Make straight the way of the Lord,'*
> as Isaiah the prophet said." (John 1:23)

**Reflection:** Writers, artists, actors and actresses, indeed all of us, seek to find our voice, that is, the words and tonality that truly express our true selves. John the Baptist found his voice. Although the words spoken in today's gospel were taken from the prophet Isaiah, they succinctly and clearly articulated his mission of preparing the way of the Lord.

Later, at the Jordan River, John the Baptist would make another proclamation. With the advent of Jesus' public ministry, he, John, had completed his work so that as his ministry would decrease, Jesus' mission would be on the ascent.

Finding our voice, finding our authentic identity and vocation, is no easy task. Too easily we can assume a false voice, uttering the words of our culture or some passing philosophy, adopting a mission that leads to death and not to life. Prayer and grace are necessary to achieve clarity regarding God's particular will in our life. Add to that, perhaps, some help from a spiritual director.

Hermann Hesse's novel *Siddhartha* (1922), a book dealing with self-discovery, speaks of the river (central metaphor of the story) as having many voices, sometimes the voice of a king or warrior, a bull or a night bird, or a pregnant woman or sighing man. We too have a variety of voices as we develop over the years and have new experiences. But there is one voice that is central to our identity and ministry and it has to be the voice of love, receiving and giving and speaking this language. When we find this voice, we become an epiphany person.

**Meditation:** How does one find one's voice? What are the voices around you that have the greatest impact on your life?

**Prayer:** Lord Jesus, may we listen to your voice and your call to discipleship. We long to do the Father's will; we long to speak the language of love and mercy. May we find our voice and use it for spreading your kingdom.

## Agnus Dei

**Readings:** 1 John 2:29–3:6; John 1:29-34

**Scripture:**
You know that he [Jesus] was revealed to take away sins,
    and in him there is no sin.
No one who remains in him sins;
    no one who sins has seen him or known him.
    (1 John 3:5-6)

**Reflection:** *Ecce Agnus Dei, qui tollis peccata mundi, miserere nobis.* John the Baptist identified Jesus as the Lamb of God, the one who takes away the sins of the world. But this knowledge of who Jesus was came gradually and received confirmation with the descent of the Holy Spirit. This was an epiphany moment for the Baptist and led him to adjust his role in the mystery of salvation. Jesus was the one who would take away our sins and conquer death; Jesus was the one to be followed and emulated.

In Bernard MacLaverty's short story "The Beginnings of a Sin," the alcoholic priest Fr. Lynch struggles to understand how sin begins, his own sin being a case in point. He does understand that sin in some way shuts God out of his life and love.

Jesus came for people like Fr. Lynch and ourselves. He came to heal our brokenness, to liberate us from our addictions, to put us on the royal road of faith, hope, and love. He is God's Lamb who has mercy on us; Jesus is the Son of God who plunges in the baptismal waters to show the way to new life.

To know Jesus is to experience the grace of God's love and mercy, often mediated through our parents, the Christian community, the Scriptures, and the sacraments. In word and action, God comes to us so that we might live life to the full; he came to give us his joy and peace.

Our prayer today: "Give us peace!" *Agnus Dei, qui tollis peccata mundi, dona nobis pacem.*

**Meditation:** Is finding the beginning of sin difficult? Is experiencing God's mercy and peace a part of your spiritual history?

**Prayer:** Jesus, Lamb of God and Son of the Father, continue to shed your mercy and peace upon us and the world. Our sins are many; our resolution so weak. Only if we are overshadowed by the Holy Spirit will we come to know you and do the Father's will.

## A Call within a Call

**Readings:** 1 John 3:7-10; John 1:35-42

**Scripture:**
John was standing with two of his disciples,
    and as he watched Jesus walk by, he said,
    "Behold, the Lamb of God."
The two disciples heard what he said and followed Jesus.
    (John 1:35-37)

**Reflection:** The call to become a disciple of the Lord comes in a variety of ways. The two disciples of John the Baptist heard a direct call from Jesus himself: "Come, and you will see." Simon Peter heard about Jesus through his brother Andrew. Saint Elizabeth Ann Seton, whose feast we celebrate today, heard her call through the hospitality and faith witness of a family she met in Italy. Jesus does pursue us "down the nights and down the days."

The invitation to discipleship involves a secondary call. We are not just to say yes to a relationship with Christ; we are also to say yes to a particular work or ministry that will further the kingdom of God. For Elizabeth Ann Bayley that call within a call was to start a school in Baltimore and eventually form a religious community, the Sisters of Charity of

St. Joseph. That community would eventually open orphanages as well as continue their educational ministry.

Whatever one's particular ministry is, all ministries will ultimately involve charity, the love of our sisters and brothers in our unique situations. Our first reading today is clear about this matter: we are to act in righteousness so as to make clear that we are children of God. Failure to act justly gives lie to the claim that we are true disciples of Jesus.

St. Elizabeth Ann Seton and her community beheld Jesus, the Lamb of God, and followed in his way of self-giving love.

**Meditation:** How did you discern your vocation, your call to follow Christ? Who were the people who mediated that call?

**Prayer:** St. Peter, St. Andrew, St. John the Baptist, St. Elizabeth Ann Seton, pray for us that we too may hear and follow our Savior. Through your intercession may we be granted the wisdom and courage to hear and answer God's call. May we one day celebrate with you the joy and peace of heaven.

## "You Get What You See!"

**Readings:** 1 John 3:11-21; John 1:43-51

**Scripture:**
Jesus saw Nathanael coming toward him and said of him,
   "Here is a true child of Israel.
There is no duplicity in him." (John 1:47)

**Reflection:** "You get what you see!" Such is seldom the case. Most of us have the innate ability to disguise our true intentions by "cleverly" using deceptive words or actions. Who has not been guilty of saying one thing to a person's face and something quite different behind that person's back?

Well, we have an exception in Nathanael. You do get what you see and Jesus stood in admiration of Nathanael's forthrightness. Although Nathanael was dead wrong about questioning whether any good could come out of Nazareth (such a "good" as the Savior, the Lord), yet Nathanael said what he thought without deception. He would go on to follow Jesus and put his guilelessness to use in furthering God's kingdom.

Peter and Judas dealt with duplicity. One denied the Lord, a Lord he journeyed with for so many miles. The other betrayed the Lord, a Lord who loved him unto death. Be it cowardice or greed, pride or fear, we are all vulnerable in failing to be true to ourselves, we who are made in God's image and likeness. Blessed is the person to whom Jesus says, "Here is a person without guile."

Maybe one of the reasons that Shakespeare is considered such a great writer is the fact that he captured human nature so well in his plays. He tells it the way it is and is especially gifted in making us see the deceitful cunning of the human heart. The mirror Shakespeare holds up to us is painful, yet, in seeing ourselves in his characters, we might be drawn to turning to the Lord for healing and honesty.

**Meditation:** Have you ever been guilty of duplicity or been the victim of duplicity? Why is total honesty about our intentions so difficult to attain?

**Prayer:** Lord Jesus, we ask for the grace of honesty and transparency. Give us new hearts so that we are able to look you in the eye. Only through the gift of your Holy Spirit will we be able to say what we truly feel and believe.

## Happenings: Big and Small

**Readings:** 1 John 5:5-13; Mark 1:7-11 or Luke 3:23, 31-34, 36, 38

**Scripture:**
It happened in those days that Jesus came from Nazareth
   of Galilee
and was baptized in the Jordan by John. (Mark 1:9)

**Reflection:** A homiletic professor asserted that if anything is to *happen* in a homily the Holy Spirit must animate the poor words of the preacher and open the hearts of the congregation. Then there is a *happening*, an event of great importance.

The Holy Spirit was at the Jordan when John baptized Jesus. And a great happening transpired as a voice was heard calling Jesus God's beloved son and affirming Jesus' mission. The great happening was the salvation of the world.

On our Christian journey we celebrate the mysteries of our creation, redemption, and sanctification every time the Eucharist happens. We give thanks for the gift of life, the gift of Jesus, our Redeemer, and the great gift of the Holy Spirit who hovers over our bent and bruised world. The same Spirit that hovered over the Jordan and Jesus hovers over us and wants us to know that we are God's beloved daughters and sons. When we appropriate this good news, we then venture forth and journey with Jesus in his mission of being agents of the Father's love and mercy.

It is especially in the small happenings of life that we further God's kingdom: the word of encouragement to a struggling coworker, the phone call to a lonely person, the note of gratitude to a second-grade teacher, a smile of recognition across the room. The Spirit animates our simple deeds and bestows peace and joy to every open heart.

**Meditation:** What are the great and small happenings in your life? What role does the Holy Spirit play in your daily transactions?

**Prayer:** Come, Holy Spirit, come. Animate our minds with truth and our hearts with affection and compassion. Make us instruments of Jesus' mission; empower us to give glory to God by our loving deeds. *Veni, Creator Spiritus.*

## **The Secret of a Good Marriage**

**Readings:** 1 John 5:14-21; John 2:1-11

**Scripture:**
There was a wedding at Cana in Galilee,
   and the mother of Jesus was there.
Jesus and his disciples were also invited to the wedding.
   (John 2:1-2)

**Reflection:** We have all been invited to a wedding where we witness the public profession of love and commitment. We have all been at wedding receptions where the wine runs free and gifts are given.

Mary and Jesus were also invited to a wedding and they delivered a gift. By providing wine, they saved the day and considerable embarrassment. Mary's homily—"Do whatever he tells you"—was short and to the point. In five words, we were given the truth about what our calling is.

Several years ago I was at a wedding reception and here is what happened:

   The banquet hall, three-hundred-guest-filled,
   rocked with laughter, loud talk, conviviality.
   Add to this good food, drink aplenty, and music.

   Suddenly there was quiet
   as the best man stood to toast the bride and groom.
   The best man shared his secret,

the secret of his marriage of twenty-two years:
"The secret of my marriage is dying to oneself!"

The silence in the hall deepened
for everyone there, deep down, knew
that the best man was delivering the wedding homily,
and he did it in nine words.

Glasses were raised,
the toast was made,
and the din continued
but not before the truth was spoken.

**Meditation:** What does Jesus tell you to do?

**Prayer:** Lord Jesus, give us the grace to reach out to those in need. May we emulate you in your compassion and generosity. Teach us to die to our selfishness so that we may, like you, be a person for others.

# EPIPHANY AND BAPTISM
## OF THE LORD

## Epiphany: The Universality of God's Love

**Readings:** Isa 60:1-6; Eph 3:2-3a, 5-6; Matt 2:1-12

**Scripture:**
Lord, every nation on earth will adore you. (Ps 72:11)

**Reflection:** God's love and mercy is universal, available to all people, to all the nations of humankind. The magi symbolize "foreigners" come to pay homage to the child born under a star. Saint Paul, called to be a steward of God's grace, proclaims with joy that the Gentiles are coheirs, copartners, and members of the same body who share in the Gospel promise. And the prophet Isaiah, centuries before the birth of Jesus, foretells God's light and glory breaking into human history. That vision would be fulfilled in Christ.

In our faith life we are called through baptism to adoration, communion, and cooperation. Adoration follows from an epiphany, a seeing of truth, goodness, and beauty. In these transcendentals, God is revealed and we are challenged to respond with worship. Every culture and every religion have aspects of goodness and beauty, of wisdom and truth. Our Christian faith claims that in Christ, the Light of all nations, the Prince of Peace, God's presence and grace is made manifest. For those who have eyes to see, adoration and praise follow.

Communion is the realization of oneness and unity. Jesus' vision is that all may be one, that division and alienation be ended. The work of redemption is the restoration of unity. Isaiah's prophecy speaks of nations walking in the light of God's glory. Saint Paul proclaims how God's promise of salvation is inclusive. Matthew's gospel speaks of the human condition and how Herod, troubled by word of a newborn king, attempted to disrupt God's plan of unity and oneness. The feast of the Epiphany is all about communion.

A third aspect of our spiritual life is cooperation. Saint Paul cooperated with the graces given him by being a steward and servant of God's mysteries revealed in Jesus. Isaiah likewise responded to his call to be a prophet and to share a vision with the people of his day and with us as well. And the magi? They brought their gifts as a confirmation that Jesus was indeed the newborn king. Cooperators one and all.

**Meditation:** Which of the three aspects of spirituality—adoration, communion, cooperation—is strongest in your life? What has God asked you to do in cooperating with the work of redemption?

**Prayer:** Jesus, Prince of Peace and Lord of Life, help us to see the mystery of your Father's love and mercy. Make manifest to us what we must do to be true disciples. Grant us the grace of loving adoration, of blessed communion, and of dedicated service. May we give you the gift of ourselves.

## Testing the Spirits

**Readings:** Isa 42:1-4, 6-7; Acts 10:34-38; Matt 3:13-17

**Scripture:**
Thus says the LORD:
Here is my servant whom I uphold,
    my chosen one with whom I am well pleased,
upon whom I have put my spirit. (Isa 42:1a)

**Reflection:** In his marvelous poem "The Negro Speaks of Rivers," Langston Hughes (1902–67) mentions the Euphrates and the Congo, the Nile and the Mississippi, but he does not speak of the Jordan. True, in comparison with the mighty rivers of the world, the Jordan River is insignificant in size, but as for spiritual importance it outrivals them all. For it was at the Jordan that the eternal Son of God identified in a powerful way with our humanity; it was at the Jordan that Jesus, the son of Mary, experienced his chosen-ness.

Those of us who were taken to the river of our church's baptismal font were given a share in the life and ministry of Christ. The Spirit came upon us as well as the commission to go and do what Jesus did: proclaim by our lives the mystery of God's love and mercy. Later, that commission would be strengthened through the grace of confirmation; later, that commission would be nourished by the reception of the Eucharist.

When couples are preparing for marriage, they are asked to obtain copies of their baptismal certificates. And there it is: a specific date, the names of their parents and godparents, the minister and place of baptism. But the baptism received years before is an ongoing sacrament: all of us are being baptized as we journey through life. The young couple will be married on a particular day, but in the weeks and years to follow they are being married. God's grace continues to nourish and call us to grow in our lives of discipleship.

At the Jordan Jesus experienced the Father's pleasure. May we, on this feast of the Lord's baptism, experience the same love of the Father.

**Meditation:** In what sense are the sacraments ongoing? Is there anything special you can do for the Lord on the anniversary of your baptism?

**Prayer:** Lord Jesus, you came to live among us in the fullness of our humanity. At the Jordan River, you experienced your mission in a special way. Help us to journey with you; help us to experience the Father's love and to share it with all we meet.

# References

*Introduction*
Francis, The Joy of the Gospel (*Evangelii Gaudium*) (Vatican City: Libreria Editrice Vaticana, 2013).

*December 17: Saturday of the Third Week of Advent*
Karl Rahner, *The Need and the Blessing of Prayer*, trans. Bruce W. Gillette (Collegeville, MN: Liturgical Press, 1997), 49.

*December 20: Tuesday of the Fourth Week of Advent*
Emily Dickinson, "I dwell in Possibility," in *The Poems of Emily Dickinson: Reading Edition*, ed. Ralph W. Franklin (Cambridge, MA: Belknap Press of Harvard University Press, 1999).

*December 21: Wednesday in Late Advent*
Gerard Manley Hopkins, "Spring," in *Poems and Prose of Gerard Manley Hopkins*, selected by W. H. Gardner (New York: Penguin, 1985).

*December 28: The Holy Innocents, Martyrs*
Benedict XVI, *Spe Salvi* (Saved in Hope) (Vatican City: Libreria Editrice Vaticana, 2007).

*December 30: The Holy Family of Jesus, Mary and Joseph*
Robert Hayden, "Those Winter Sundays," in *Collected Poems*, ed. Frederick Glaysher (New York: Liveright Publishing, 2013).
Flannery O'Connor, "Greenleaf," in *The Complete Stories* (New York: Farrar, Straus and Giroux, 1971), 329.